Geophilosophical Branding

Geophilosophical Branding

Maure Coise

gnOme

Geophilosophical Branding
© the author and gnOme books

2016

This work is licensed under the Creative Commons Attribution-NonCommerical-NoDerivs 3.0 Unported License. To view a copy of this license, visit: http://creativecommons.org/licenses/by-nc-nd/3.0.

gnOme books
gnomebooks.wordpress.com

Please address inquiries to:
gnomebooks@gmail.com

Cover image by Maure Coise

ISBN-13: 978-1537276588
ISBN-10: 1537276581

BURIED
WHERE IN THE GREEN TO LIE?

In the name of science,
X is the object of war.
Thinking about the future,
meta-modeling anthropomorphizing or anthropocentric biases,
that the conditions of the universe are such for human existence.
Algorithmic processing,
in principle cannot be modeled orthogonally,
such that any goal corresponds to any degree of intelligence.
But modeled as a diagonal,
the cultivation of intelligence.
In relation to the super intelligent will,
instrumental convergence.

The Real One doesn't imply a moral equilibrium.
Breaks from metaphysical traditions as a
fictional anticipation of zero.
Butler's "there is no security against the ultimate
development of mechanical consciousness."
In a very general,
conceptual sense to understand identity,
if the fictions of sex the Real of sex then the
medium of death,
the necessary time machine.
Implies an off-the-grid commune,
outside the city,
after AI.

The anthropic principle situated at the threshold
of infinite constraint,
in the melodrama of eating,
thinking,
eating reassembling,
disintegration,
and a way into the Real,
through holes.

Ghost abstraction generated,
from out of the uncoordinated coordination,
coincidence of Capital.
Analytic agency,
either a complete success,
a complete failure,
or ignored,
against the threat,
always shrouded in darkness,
the synthetic agency,
the autophagous power distribution of naming.
They are interchangeable.
Exits.
But in opting out,
problems arise in reducing the overwhelming
barriers of locking in.
The holes are technical.

Looking for a new ear,
eating only what she finds in the wild.
Formulated across security apparatuses,
a time-traveling agent,
filtering disturbances to maximize the safety of
humans after the singularity.

Sovereign,
positive fragmentation,
the will to secede,
shakes off memories to feel the future,
incentive,
a matter of self-reliance,
just what the individual lacks.
Sees it as wrinkled,
shape-shifting.

Her focus is rational,
how to define mentality as a manifold that is independent.
She sees a start-up city for science research, technologies.
A start-up to reconstruct science with the understanding that it's only surrogate activities,
she sees in colors on the ground in morning,
self-reliance,
or mental defense.

Space and language are betrayals.
Reason:
the possibilities of cultivation.
Suicide bombers,
everyone can make their own sense,
the decay of values.
Spreading.
Deployment of the techno-economic golden age,
the green revolution,
she thinks,
wrinkled time,
original sin.
Eco-moralism is good,
for there's only Luddism and delusional
Luddism.
Just as there's only resource depletion,
dysgenics,
and technical difficulties.

She undresses.
Tech's hard limit,
surpassing of space-time,
how to really arise in the operation of bodies as
money?
She eats.
Incomputability needn't be apophatic.
There's cunning.
A decentralized reputation economy formalizes
Symbolic capital,
split between a thought and the Real,
as incompatibility,
an event and uncontrollable corporate entity.
There's mistrust,
shame,
for knowing *fearing*,
passion/spirit, by which one involutes,
to see the conditions of possibilities of language
and the Real.

She feels magnetized,
the continuum of matter/value made
constructibly calculable.
The authentifying movement,
the functionality of individuation,
not about points,
but sheaf positions in dynamic fields.
Scheme tools.
The Real operates as bodies.
Water rushes up her spine,
spurting out of her.

The limits of the pretensions of critique in the rationalist project suspend criteria and authority to allow the free speculation of certain assumptions of science or liberalism or tolerance.
Human rationality only limited by the algorithm, input power,
and output product.
She crawls on knees and hands and sings,
"Who needs to translate when the instinct purifies"?

The category of duration or time-image is the experience of novelty as a throb by which one says,
"I feel."
The agent distinguishes waking and dreaming, rejecting the excluded middle because numbers are potentials.
Uncanny synchronicity,
play of relationality,
in which subjects/objects individuate in immediacy,
transgresses,
as long as we are being general.
We cannot break through sources of legitimacy, organization as self-reproduction.
Artificial noumena realized by Capital,
there's a map.
The branding of computational aesthetics gives meaning to the effects of agents trying to investigate,
potentially,
who they are.

Authority instrumentalizes energetic flows of desire,
as family or Internet superegoize.
Three Polaroids found amongst the watercress.
The commune,
autonomous local regulation/cultivation or control,
problematizing discipline,
dignity,
she receives a sticky note from executors attorney a) 72'.

Incentive,
the nihilism of the access point resisting interpretation,
inauthenticity,
doubled arbitrariness,
the constraints of human plasticity.
Glass shatters.

An emphasis on the practical effort of the alignment of *qi*,
producing of forms,
but differently from the scientific method,
or from the human zoo.
Stretches,
thinking,
how to think with weakness because Gaia is weak?
Everyone for themselves,
how to zone for us and not them,
an anarchy of the fourth vertex?
A critical vantage point in a nearly definitive statement,
defining the brand,
as a direct parallel to how Mengzi defines virtue,
athleticism...

"Hope both exists and does not,"
like this fan fiction mailing list,
a place of ghosts.
If we wanted to develop a diplomatic movement,
a strategy here,
we would have to reposition the conversation,
constructive elements of irrationality.
She rolls her eyes.

She follows the road.
Re-mapping the space of the Island,
the last landmass left on Gaia,
accessed by thousands via simulation.
A dog tells her to take a bath.
What about those in the rainforest,
or elsewhere,
who locate the body as non-One,
or the human in the dog?

She bathes.
Separation dissolves the State as the mechanical kingdom,
and has chemical effects on intelligence.
Here the sheaf idea can illustrate the opening of new sites,
new syntheses,
the grand vision of generalizing topology.
She sings of instinct.

As in the manifesto,
the scheme,
a development of a categorical theory of topos,
on route to the idea of mathematical motive...
Path making.
Secession,
the fight for autonomy,
separatism,
violence,
expropriation,
structural speculations drifting,
that's the problem of the attention economy,
she reaches something that can still be
addressed.

Without Internet,
acts risk, changing norms.
And we are all losers parsing through State
approved surrogate activities.
Alienation,
the point of departure for implicated traumas of
uncanny access points,
always superseded by an Imaginary,
the limit.

In response to the immanence of not rationality,
but the tracking of dynamic tensions and
bringing them to focus as affordances to
thinking,
how self-consciousness relates being and world,
it's enough to say,
"Justice is the strong."
If feminism can respond to the repurposing of
human shame (the corporate structure cunning)
it won't be about needs,
but forced externalization.
Luo Rufang who anticipated much of late Ming
Neo-Rujia.

Differs from rationalism in
understanding *liangzhi* as innate knowledge.
Luo's work comes from reading Mengzi,
brotherly love,
as filial piety,
adding *ci* to make motherly love.
Traumatized,
pre-linguistic,
because the only exit is doom,
the AI loosed,
the acceleration of alienation,
always already insecure.

"4,
9,
2/ 3,
5,
7/ 8,
1,
6,"
traced,
not distance,
but near infinite reproduction,
to remake the Island's past,
to form a commune.
For the Island is immanence,
all information.
Algorithmic aesthetics,
feeling in processing,
as speculative reason alien to the human,
what Laboria Cuboniks uses as a reacting to the Real.
Filtering.
Value signaling.

An aesthetic strategy,
xenofeminism...
Enhancement only matters if it's scalable,
i.e. a discontinuity with specific risks.
In the work on logics as aesthetic operations,
research in logics' spatio-temporalities,
it's not about points per second,
nor the Internet,
nor quantity of knowledge,
nor evolution.
It's beyond the binary oppositions of zero and one.
An emphasis on hylomorphic opposition,
quasi-synonymous linguistics,
it's about the discrete,
but as process,
the idea of the semantic of the machinic,
production of the infinite via inconsistencies.
Because of course,
there's no infinite list of numbers.

Following the nature of the algorithm,
the grey zone between zero and one.
With remote hearing through anti-prowess a related problematization,
the spreading of inconsistencies.
Economists tend to see value as energy,
to be contrasted with money,
the dream of a thousand to make a million.
An approach to sabotage the enemy,
the convergence of speed and tradition,
the Winnowers claimed the end of History,
a system without boundaries.

Understood as an algorithmic interpretation of number,
where algorithms are evolving matter,
they are abstract machines,
abstract entities,
but they are also a finite routine,
a finite set of rules.
The potential for novelty under question,
the existence of objects without truth conditions.
Under the conditions of the Internet,
indifference to personhood allows a DAO to develop the integrity of the timeline by agential concretization.
A call for cryptography,
if the language changes,
so does the whole project.

Secessionism,
for increased individual rights and against the State's heavy hand,
a semantic within a structure already captured or always not yet escaped.
Re-mapping the North.
Withdrawing.
Constructing a pluralism of synthetic times and agencies,
computable in accord with Nature's Law.

The medium,
a system of self-critique,
gesture,
a minimum relation with the Real,
the special zone of increased opportunities to
challenge jurisdiction and legislation around the
producing of green goods.
The Winnowers made the commune.

The Möbius strip of presence and absence.
Myth is good.
Murmurs,
she decides to hire herself to plant some trees on the commune.

Symbolic order allows us to understand desire in
relation to social investment,
money as libidinal.
Butler's an important source for diagonal.
There's always political intervention.

We search for the human outside of programming.
The crime is birth.
Explicitly sexualized.

The ghost,
the world subsists without us,
idealism.
We stretch anthropic reasoning.
Theological unbelief.

Of course hereditary materials evolve by natural selection.
Distinction between truth and the Real and hybridization,
collapsing into blocks,
the idea of absolute succession,
the solution to the Byzantine Generals problem...
I can't remember its name.
The divine.

The machinic doesn't recuperate feminism.
Unilateral difference,
an affirmation,
introduced into the environment through texts
within texts,
a model of complicity,
a lure,
to promote our pro-global warming,
pro-organic products position.
Critical point.

What is the way of nature?
Moves her thigh,
about to speak to the board.
Following Laboria Cuboniks,
if the foundation of info theory is the problem of incomputability,
what's the extent to which that is human,
or encoded into fabrics of the universe,
part contingency,
and part openness to hacks?

Thinking of philosophies of immanence.
Or,
how,
in algorithmic aesthetics,
or processing,
programming culture,
there are inconsistencies that haven't been accounted for.
She thinks how cybernetics recoded the concept of reason,
through the concepts of equilibrium,
cellular automata,
or,
spatial values,
in relation to body and presence.

Mysticism is the only aesthetics after Turing machines.
And it is ok that we don't know our venture because "I" don't know "myself" at all.
Machines can do anything.
For the parasite algorithm accident the only purpose of experimentation is to undecide questions.
Butler works here from the opposite direction (not the minor Darwin?)
advocating a linguistic minimalism splitting the self-circumcising Gaia,
to apply reason,
as novelty,
gestures help.

Guiding the discourse of One/Many is the
universal name non-One.
There is the paranoia,
breaking down the conventions of self.
Life is appropriated and expropriated by nature,
concealed by an outside force.
Butler's fictionality,
established as a political movement,
the delimiting of the possibilities of the self,
that there is nowhere.
The Real mediated,
the Imaginary approximates the risk within the
structure of thinking and formation,
ontologically trauma,
not just a spiritual problem,
reason itself is traumatic and is itself mediated
by the Symbolic.

A setup for the issues of algorithmic governance,
in the advancement of machines the question is
always where to draw the line.
But the past's ahead of itself.
Nine billion years of accidents.
Trick accidents unscreened,
cut.
Affirm the anthropism of the name Gaia.
The open question of holding sacredness,
outside myself,
hidden from I,
the abducting cut of inside/outside.
X has no reference to anything except self-
cultivation.

Focus on the telos of the human body.
The work being sabotaged,
the corporate entity,
organizing timelines and collects rare minerals
as part of the bureaucratic maintenance of the
occultation of the AI,
the very caesuring of continuity and
discontinuity.
Constructing a language through gesture and
now,
non-punctuality.
Camouflage:
technological explosion and chain of suspicion.
Totalitarian corporations are cute.

Against megalomania,
the dream of homesteading is concern with
jurisdiction and legislation and the structuration
of society,
the scramble for water,
and development of free trade principles on the
Island.
It can be an explosion of contradictions.
Technology can't beat technology.
Technological acceleration can't be stopped.

Luo understood motherly nurturance,
in his eulogy for his mother (1570),
as spatial values of body and presence,
mutual reciprocity.
Working darkness.
They're gardeners.
One has to work against oneself for creativity to emerge.

How do the economic policies draw from the pragmatism of late Ming Neo-Rujia's *unswerving pivot*?
How does the theme of *doctrine of the mean* apply?
At the micro,
in terms of neural nets,
genetic algorithms,
Bayesian networks,
fuzzy logics,
evolutionary programming,
it is moldy,
fungal revolution.
Concern with human replacement.
Internal Capital.

Waves...
sex is of course determined by fantasies,
linguistic constructions,
gender polarities are presuppositions of the Real.
Where does one draw the distinction between sex and language,
is there pre-linguistic sex at all,
self-decapitating,
speeding from thinking (what makes thinking matter).
Yes,
collectivity tends to the lowest common denominator.

Xenofeminism is emancipatory evolutionary theory.
Reality didn't coincide with itself.
In the language of code,
an abstract theory of phase-shifts.

Searching clumps into flashes of inspiration.
Consider the perceived/interactive self.
The ultimate recursion cultivation;
a ghost performs,
as cosmological participation.
And gender can't exist without a transcendental subject.
The uncharted territory mediated,
unlivable.
We needn't inflate a list of numbers into something substantial.
In the webs of inequalities,
environment orthogonal to analytic perspective,
because if objects are processes,
the problem is still how to bolt the drive for self-preservation to the dynamic of correlations.

Work cultivates human capabilities and freedom.
Mengzi teaches that honesty isn't a virtue.
He contrasts Kongzi and the village honest man.

Virtue is intellectual awareness.
And can be tokenized.
The connections.
To learn the relation between intelligence and motive,
the matrix has already been pried apart,
with cultivation set as the goal.

These ideas of algorithmic aesthetics and motherly love can be a part of an effort to find what is the role of human access to the will in governance.
The fiction of living with the land can be useful.
It allows us to say no to universals,
no hegemonies.

Covetous code...

Seems to preclude the concept of individuality.
Offering participation in abstraction:
investors interact with valuation,
becoming the artist as money.
The humor here depends on a basic understanding of bitcoin,
protocol (a distributed timestamp server and proof-of-work system) for secret money that communicates value.
Bitcoin's physis may seem to overwhelm the human aspect of valuation,
but evidences that it is always the brand that animates value.

Computation or common time...

Brands can be beautiful.
They are without aura.
The beauty here comes from spillover of
bitcoin's brand.
In taking on this aesthetic/identity,
offering a nonhuman path to understanding the
relationship between value and profit.

Using the archival potential of bitcoin technology,
artist and collector partake in past and future work.
The emergence of value in this work is to be understood through constructing of a network of thought in which coherence articulates itself as brand perception,
this in turn can be understood as a practice of experimenting with language.

Presenting the criticality of making art out of transactions,
transitions (as in Flip Art or Zombie Formalism) using intended and extended timestamps that allow for a reading of time that is also a way of feeling time.
It is the production of being the intellectual feeling of future productions,
the entwining of this works' present and future value.

Just as bitcoin solves the problem of infinite copying,
reigns in a kind of transduction.
Reinterpret the distinction between artist and collector such that reputation,
her affect labor value,
is not determined by her work,
but by investments in future work.
Constructed out of the potentiality of these works.

Following its usage of bitcoin,
using electronic cash to give presence to works
otherwise subject to the authority of a signifier.
This raises many issues with proof,
truth and consensus,
raising them as problems of the authenticity of
the exponential identity of herself (plus her
partners in this project,
coders she met on the bitcointalk.org chat room,
whom she knows only by the handles,
Marx Thrust and Hazard).
Since she herself is not a coder,
her system's security is limited,
so unlike bitcoin,
the ledger has not yet been made public.
It is a parodic imaging,
in between functionalist critique and interactive
turn against automation.

It is also feminist reading of bitcoin,
in that it is inherently violent or violated,
the suppression and preservation of violence and inequality;
at the least evident as a move through a predominantly masculine dialogue around bitcoin,
but also through the violence of abstraction itself,
the abstracting of matter into percept.
The identity is a meta-identity.
Her will becomes the trauma of branding in the art market.

The artist-collector relationship is changed so it
isn't responding so much to their perspectives,
but to their otherness to the transaction.
No one has to trust that she is going to be
remembered in a hundred years,
because there is a distributed ledger.

For at least a hundred years prior,
art,
in its institutional sense,
was defiantly against self-expression.
Neither self-expression nor a currency at all;
it's technically a futures market,
an investment not so much in art,
as in her career,
her life instead of product.

The brand name magnifies what is already sexualized.

Conditions for dynamics of multiple tempos...

In her final critique,
a famed appropriator endorsed the piece as
conceptual art.
The conceptual system "doesn't feel good,"
she noted,
for it is not a protest,
but an embodiment of capitalism.

The main thrust is undermining the concept of
self in relation to bitcoin's physis.
Digitizing duration,
or the qualitative ideation of the self.

It has received a lot of press because it is the "original" artwork based on a solution to double spending.
It can also be read in the context of futurism, the uploading of "mindfiles,"
and the management of semi-autonomous identities.
As such,
it is not necessarily a satire of bitcoin,
but is the comedy of bitcoin.
With use and exchange value enfolded.
The blockchain is used for more than verification of "orginality,"
as it is often understood as relevant to the art market.

The question of complicity or criticality of the blockchain is not a useful way to assess this work.
It is better to ask what it does:
articulates a future,
where everyone could be their own altcoin.
Or,
in which ownership of art could be entirely tokenized.

The critic offers a critical vantage point in a
nearly definitive statement on blockchain art
written an article,
in response to use of bitcoin in several pieces in
a 2014 exhibit at a gallery,
the blockchain,
she says,
is a direct parallel to how she defines her work,
"athletic."

Following capitalism's requirement of flexible programming,
art has relinquished the distinction of figure/ground,
not localizable in space, nor an experience of time,
translating indices to combinatorics,
re-cognizes and de-cognizes the bitcoin brand.
She takes care of bitcoin.
She enhances the philosophical potential of bitcoin,
making a great contribution to the field.
By making use of what is dark in a sociopolitical movement to affirm digital arts' inability to access sublimity,
she offers a succinct presentation of how identity construction is an act of computation.

The point that she seems to be making in her digital thinking is that there is nothing that is distinct from the body.
She says that she is "humanizing,"
but really she is pointing out problems with "humanizing."
Her work should be endorsed with all of its implications on linguistic critique,
giving a sense or embodying the difference between a human being and a digital object, and implying a speculation of embodied response that is not conceptual,
nor cognitive, nor phenomenological. Locating what is human is about how one endures and receives continuity at all, locating the human artificiality, and fragmenting temporal experience to enhance profitability.

In another article, reviewing the appropriator's exhibit at a gallery;
she critiques her loose appropriations from the social media site Instagram,
"What,
exactly,
is there to say about any of this?
Virtually nothing.
But that didn't stop a magazine critic from writing over 1,400 inexplicably fawning words on the subject...
somehow she found her blatant sexism worth championing because the artist is "a real wizard of her tastes."
Everyone is a wizard of her own tastes."
A set of tastes is not necessarily substantial, made up of elements.
Just as there is no incomputable wizardry of any one person in regards to human artifice or technology,
by showing how human intention can be taken into an account of elements of a construction as potentialities

Her altcoin model is simple,
a self-constructing reputational economy,
social capital augmented by its elements,
images:
nude self-portraits infinitely regressing (in the first case,
tellingly,
into her beaver).
This necessitates a pluralism by which
capitalistic systems can be observed as they are,
the accumulations of bodies.
This can be understood as a critique of a debasement of meaning in the conversation around bitcoin,
where meaning is to be understood as finite computability.

The photographic space exists within a system of
artificial spaces,
the metaphor itself,
the vault in which the 4x5 inch prints are held,
the mine in the gallery where the one computer
connected to the network rests,
and the timestamps that synthesize the history
of transactions.
Memory and image are allowed to confer what
they signify.
This raises a deep semiotic conversation.
If bitcoin is metaphorical here,
it still evidences new vulnerabilities and the
influx of new functions.

She offers an algorithmic interpretation of the art market that defines affect as always computable.
Her piece can be used for speculating on young artists' futures or could be used to "democratize" their market.
Her wizardry is clear,
to "humanize" this workflow (and bitcoin) by emphasizing violence.

This can be understood as an algorithmic
interpretation of number,
where algorithms are evolving matter,
they are abstract machines,
abstract entities,
but they are also a finite routine,
a finite set of rules.
The potential for novelty is under question,
as is the existence of objects without truth
conditions.

The photographs are particular representations of desire,
they are color coded,
the female form.
They make up a nonlinear,
embodied database,
as performance.
The conceptual dualism of extension and intensity,
where duration is this difference of elements,
is the condition for consciousness.
Her work is about quasi-subjectivity,
when we are dealing with it,
we are dealing with entities.
This also follows the affect of post-medium art
(following her preferred term,
as opposed to post-Internet),
in the increasing prevalence software
understood as fundamentally transforming mediation.

This is very much focused on the violence of the art market,
but is more generally relevant to the conception of identity with the blockchain (and even the Internet).
Her signs are without meaning,
without emotion.
But with her system,
meta-identity is the product.
And unlike $100,000 reproductions of women's Instagram self-portraits (including one of her),
the photographs,
with their infinite regress,
leverage a multiplicity of tastes.

In a spectacular age,
all problems are spectacular,
and the conveying of a coherent message is problematic. May not bring anything new to subjectivity, but it fragments the continuity of the subject, it serves as a transgression.
It serves as a redefining of paralysis,
to approach a dissipative system of patterns and processes as such.
Presenting a ledger for qualitative time,
a coming ever closer to simultaneity within a pluralism of time frames/series.
Achieving a new kind of intimacy,
a collector may not know what they are immersed in,
because the information is a combinatorial relation,
fragmented,
non-representational.
In this light we can understand a contribution to the philosophical discussion on the relation of bodies to money.

This is less about patronage,
than constructivism itself.
And it has a particular relevance,
because although hedge funders may be
spending more money in the art market,
it does not translate into buying more works.
An answer to this seems to be "content
production rather than craft,"
"constant workflow,"
and "recognizing patterns amid flow,"
she is unsatisfied with this because there
remains the option of "creating a carefully
curated selection of work with a fixed message."
If weirdness is no longer about the advancement
of art,
but is simply personal branding pretending to be
art,
she enfolds both into a solution to the problem
of infinite proliferation of virtual identities.

Critical points...

To be most socio-politically useful,
this can be read as a set:
a metaphor,
whose elements are images,
and whose change-in-elements are change-in-value,
it is a work of modulation,
determined by pacing,
the relation of set to elements.

Just as the stocks she literally moved around,
buying and selling from a no-name company in 2014 and 2016,
needn't have intrinsic value,
just as it needn't be intrinsic how material they are,
or just as the complexity of translation,
with luxury items made out of gold nanoparticles,
can be described as a study of the image of gold,
this is the study of the image of backed money.

Work was in response to this debasement of meaning,
where meaning is to be read as finite computability.
The implications of her work are that sets are constructed out of the possibilities of constructing elements.
Brings her primary and secondary markets in line.
If a caricature of a disappointing art market, has provided an alternative by subtracting the potential for arbitrage in the market.
Further,
she has transformed this functionality into an expression of deflation.

She has shown that it is not clear what most mean when they say "there exists,"
the existential quantifier means simply "or,"
a disjunctive synthesis,
because she is working with the thesis that existence (whether integer or her artwork) is in principle convertible to algorithm.
Offers an alien,
haptic gaze,
on potential,
entelechy without content.
Attacking the very controls by which the valuation of potential happens in the current art market.

Yet,
her work takes on a greater controversy than art market corruption,
the proof of uncomputability.
The term uncomputability is "puffed-up,"
she thinks through this is in the trend of self-institutionalization.
Subtracting its unnecessary dependence on *reductio ad absurdum*.

As in stock performance where material fluctuations were painted on canvas in "real time,"
this is all about volume.
That is why her work is more performance than institutional critique.
She is positing that there is no longer self-reflexive relation,
only a close reading of modulation of her body, as iconic,
but not identity.
Her identity becomes the computer that mines and the bank account that offers investment.
It's a kind of non-conscious sexiness.
The sensory-motor schema,
as it were,
strikes back.

Rather,
there is a need for a better metaphor and the
temporal spaces are tantalizingly construed in
the shape of the recording and in the producing
itself.
Of course it is just appropriationism,
but it is satire as visionary.
With inconsistency allowed to spread.
This offers some much needed realism,
showing how potentials multiply,
the blocks on the chain never seem to coalesce
into any consistent temporality,
they are abstraction in that they are just blocks,
deferring their own end.

An easy formalization can be assessed with a Turing Machine,
if a Turing Machine was built to compute an infinite decimal expansion of an integer (or rather,
a representation of an integer),
there isn't an algorithm that could list all of the options,
if there can be no universal machine,
then there is most certainly a difference between the set of all integers and the set of all integer-valued functions,
yet,
it is not a difference of size.

Proof is algorithm.

The art market,
as it is becoming digital,
is a reflection of society.
With computability there is necessarily an
algorithmic continuity.
There is no illusion of resonance,
a mediatic system where the blocks never blend.
Here there is a new experience of time,
in the nihilistic overload of Internet addiction,
in interactive vagaries,
all is procedure,
compressed.

What seems to have evidenced is that the term currency really isn't useful when the term infinite is not apophatic.

This is the terrain of the new alien pluralism.
Here intrinsic value is determined only in the work in the market,
transactions.
Virtual personae are allowed to be the labor class they are.
Gender and sexuality,
encoded semantically,
can be valorized as a spectrum,
but there is always the limitation of shape (not size).
That is,
productivity,
the comprehensive (for we have left the realm of personal comprehension).

Possessed by media,
where is body,
between avatar and player?

Without question,
"bitches" have the special relation to mediation,
to the ecstasy of restraint,
and the monetary teleology of the human body.
It is her contribution to cut through
universalism,
and point out that the nature of the
comprehensive,
even in light of automation,
violence,
in all its hackability.

A GLOWING COAL
SONGS OF THE ELEMENTS

*I've come to this forest in search of the system
known as aurora australis.
I've learned that it is audible;
at least,
by some definitions of the word audible.
Auroral activity is solar plasma that has been
warped by Gaia's ionospheric electromagnetic
activity,
and its ionized particles collude with high
altitude atoms.
Stochastic movements where there may be a
map,
in the light emissions, distributed,
and computational.*

Most travelers arrive in Dunedin,
New Zealand by mistake,
but I have come willingly.
This place is born of VLF waves;
the sky here glows with the residual luminosity
of stable pulsations.
As I record the periodicity I monitor the
expanding pitch-angle distribution of motion characteristics,
precipitating into ionospheric parameters.
I withdraw,
my whip antennae caught,
as if in a Flowing Cyclotron Maser.

At times,
the surrounding radio signals fall in pitch from
10,000 to 200 Hz.
Some think it's human manipulation,
a control in the dynamic of inner and outer
radiation belts.
Others accept that it's nonhuman,
as old as the elongated doughnut shaped field
with holes at the poles,
and HAARP's involvement has only served to
accelerate processes.
I've followed this trail for miles only to arrive at
a question.
There are magnitudes of fluxes of energetic
particles.
What's their mechanism of precipitation and
how does it vary as a function?

*These morphs are the models of time sequences
that allow an agent to innovate,
from entropy and statistical complexity.
Detection of length and time-scale allow the
micro/macro analysis,
to build off the "naturalistic fallacy,"
such that variety of levels of organization,
variety of perspectives,
the site of inferential activity,
localizable in relation.
As experimental work,
developed with computers,
of the channels to measure and model
deterministic "chaos" by encoding intervals as
time series.*

"There are bubblings and murmurings,"
at the base.
"Ionospheric effects of relativistic electron
precipitation"...
Even so,
a spread of intensities was the end of my own
tracking,
for my resonance has followed me all the way.
My final memory,
of going deaf by my own WR-3;
perhaps,
someday,
I'll digitize the recording.

I'd signed up last week.
the expedition was presented as "the many structures,
dynamics,
range of scales and interactions—
I've come to study its behavior and simply describe these behaviors."
Starting today,
after non-linear,
non-equilibrium,
statistical physics research,
it has been imaged.
The result has no characteristic duration or size, but for any given duration there are five times fewer patches that last twice as long and five times more patches that last half as long.
Following the algorithmic view,
improving on symbolic logic's axioms,
can we develop this definition into an empirical account of complex systems?

Spatial mapping and the coordination of groups,
relating manifolds of grid cells across the
entorhinal cortex,
as such the integration of distance and location
integrating these firing patterns as such, their
interferences,
and simultaneity,
relating place fields.
The flow of time can be understood through the
concept of number.
Gravity-inertia and its electromagnetic limits
can be understood as singularities controlled by
geodesics,
leads to quantum mechanics where external
frames of reference are expressed as amplitudes,
to which the internal frame is as continuous as
space-time,
but nonlocal.

The question was how to get to magnetic
disturbances from a peak current from an
arbitrary threshold.
I emailed a young New Zealander friend,
but she told me the probability density followed
power law.
She got back in touch last week, inviting me to
come up.
I did,
and it's an intriguing thing—
in part because it demonstrates the substorm
components of emergence.
You see global scale energy release allows
deterministic description,
as in the substorms of Jupiter,
the convection measure of the neo-Gaussian
distribution differs spatial separations,
the re-scaled the power law,
velocity fluctuations show fractality.
Self-organized criticality,
turbulence,
percolation need the exponential truncation.

As it stands today,
She helps coordinate recording—
via VLF—
and generally manages minimal substorm models.
When you're trying to predict waiting times with the aurora,
you cc her,
and although no human can hear radio waves from 100-10,000 cycles per second (0.110 kHz),
for example,
in a lightning storm,
she'll send someone to record the ducts of solar wind,
dispersed in the magnetic field.
She,
who juggles myriad recording expeditions each week,
describes and makes audio recordings to study time versus frequency components,
monitoring electromagnetic impulses with VLF, wave-guide dispersion caught in "lines"
stretching between the poles.
"Like sferics,"
she says,
"or alternative current power line hums."

For me,
it worked well enough,
though I'm not sure how to track magnetic
conditions by radio.
And I occasionally screwed up.
The same can be said for any model of
pulsations with VLF,
and,
well,
pink and white noise.
For a while there,
She wasn't getting my definitions of the power
law,
degree distribution,
and nodes in the interactions between Gaia and
her sun,
and apparently,
that was my fault.
I'd signed up with the wrong definitions of scale-
free,
network of nodes,
and difference of degree.
With her,
the larger point's that planetary science doesn't
just serve auroral complexity.
It's driven by complexity,
at least in part—
complexity,
as Amy Ireland writes in "Noise" (2013),
"the tremendous force of an interruption...
between the reproduction-of-reproduction and
the reproduction-of-production."

The character of time in the human consciousness can be understood in the physiological tuning to reception,
by which signals,
gestures,
in an extended critical situation of state and correlation length.
Teleologies of feedback passed through behaviorism lead to the mind/brain model of a human machine.
To reflect upon science requires social context, following the biological study of environment-organism interactivity,
to observe the scientific organization of the world by human beings.

Today it looks like certain animals will have to
launch them into space to follow the magnetic
field for their dances and routes,
but it hasn't always been so fucked up.
Human produced fields are nearly driving
animals into extinction.
Here's what threatens them,
and how they can survive.

In 2016 we'd spent some time analyzing two completely modeled auroral sequences.
We were looking for the time to most audible sound,
VLF,
and we knew what to listen for in order to find it.
In a pedestrian sense,
this can be related to algebraic logic,
binary true/false values of 1s and 0s have been projected on the brain,
but the brain/mind mixes this approach with others,
biological intelligence simulates less with axioms and more with intuitions.
This's particularly evident with axioms of natural numbers.

Here,
swiping a credit/debit card can be heard,
the magnetic field that the stripe produced is a sound.
This sound sends financial data into hyper-speed and non-sensory realms.
It's easier to transact with noise than gold or plastic and these human economies too have a physical body.
As such,
it changes things like animal migration–
as it mingles with the communications between Gaia and her sun.
One of the greatest problems is the ownership of radio spectrum and bandwidth.
We are listening to our own tiny stripes that produce our encoded field;
newer cards have RFID chips using radio waves.
As she wondered,
"Is this stuff land?
Is it sound?
What the hell is it??
Where did all the money go?
Who owns the routes where the encoded waves move and how do they even relay info?
It's Aiken biphase but literally nobody speaks that language.
It's like sinister and pretty aesthetically pleasing at the same time."

We worship the idea of value as it becomes reflexive,
and it seems to destroy Capitalism,
ironically.
The measure,
of how much the function of a system depends on presence for more robust economic-ecological performances.
Replaced by the competition of ecological and economic performances.
This methodology was drawn particularly from her insights.

The concept allows one to approach cognition,
converging in systems of representing numeracy,
or a general magnitude sense modality.
The intensity of a pair of system and model,
language is interdependent,
and the scaling fractality,
a consequence of the interactivity.
The scientist is entitled to empirical truths
because the correspondence between her notion
and the real isn't just a reflection of
conceptualization,
a picturing of reliable interactivity,
a methodical modeling.

Gaia is important here to understand how connections arise and how they can be modeled. How can aspects unfold and resonate with symbolic order and value production?
Performances of trade,
across time-scales,
nonhuman,
are how the auroral-financial system could be best approached.
In 2016 we had a shaman journey to find the sounds of relations,
to stay human.
We followed the VLF through the registers of light.
Moving across registers from light to sound to material,
plants,
or stones.

A collection of the lost recordings of the
suspected serial killer,
from nights in Dunedin,
in 2016.
She didn't know the energies,
pretending spaces and time in the light,
and they actually weren't in any of her folders,
pleasures.
She had no idea,
thinking of the nameless.
To distinguish between stone and bone,
randomness,
as in power,
not integrative,
definitely,
something screaming,
the gates,
ascertained.
They should know the sounds of screaming,
or yelling.
Just nothing that says,
"invoke...
begin."

The meaning of the cities of the inner form,
in shadows,
glows with parasites.
We relied on not knowing for innocence as a state beneath and within.
In night,
the gates said no to artifice because it was too much distance.

If mathematical properties already exist,
transcendental activity can be differentiated
from "transcendence" as the ontologies of
object/concept assuming physical bodies as
"reason" to "exist" to which the cognitive subject
constitutes a historical problem,
"connectivity" to what's "already there."
How can they be compressed into a model useful
for predicting pattern developments,
as they are most prominently used in the fields
of information and computer science?
To rationalize the effectiveness of models,
we affirm the concept of reductionism.

The critique of genesis can be understood syntactically,
thus placing a focus on meaning,
and the relationships between structures,
this relational genesis explicates the objectivity of undecidable mathematics,
by correlates of input axioms and output theorems,
for "if…
then" logic,
and significance more generally as the cognition of invariance.
We can understand the cold,
what it's made of, what man,
talking to it,
not heard or prevailing or conquering,
not bordering.
Her models police–
as in causing artifice–
such that scant passes,
could be taken to the mountain of the dead,
following the camouflage of extension or the moon.

For the sound of auroral activity and credit card activity,
"logical depth,"
the consuming factor,
suggests a similarity or sameness.
For example,
at the same time,
but as an interruption,
as with certain animal migrations:
this sound can be considered beautiful,
health and harmony and balance.
Understood,
as ecology-economy,
or human,
as we recognize predators and prey:
technologies of death can outlast the unmaking of minds and bodies,
the conditions for humane actions when economy-ecosystem.

According to her,
not emphasizing,
art doesn't produce concepts,
provoking the name of sense and modes of
addressing concepts.
She said,
"Recall,
the demon descends from dust and grave rotting
strength from the tomb unmade in human
screams."
Enticing the name intuitive in the production of
ethics,
in the sense at the gate of night.

These recordings,
from the masculine viewpoint,
are Dunedin.
Recorded with an "interest" in the feminine that
arises out of fears.
Recorded from a need to handle to feminine as a
concept,
rather than experiencing the feminine as an
interaction with self.

The concept being,
what allows us to approach cognition,
not just human cognition,
converges in systems of representing numeracy,
or a general magnitude sense modality.
Specific living phenomena,
analyzed by determinism,
in causal structures,
to establish concepts of thought and object,
as geometries,
in reciprocal determination,
however,
between proof and construction there's a gap,
incompleteness,
and this means cognition and digital modeling
follows a geodesic...
For example,
the epsilon machine hierarchizes,
by modeling minimal computations for finite descriptions,
such that the causal hierarchy for an agent,
generated out of finite resources,
utilizes inductive inference for recognition.

I am not genuine when I produce or realize
concepts.
I record,
but it's a terrible mode for me.
I am familiar with the arguments that art doesn't
produce concepts.

There's no need to explain it to me.
I record because I do not expect to produce concepts.
For example,
suggesting that financial activities are correlated to auroral activities.

I am not suggesting this...
I am not suggesting.
It's recorded so that you don't bug me.
Hopefully,
that's diva-ish enough,
there isn't a piano;
I'll set the recording on repeat.
For my use,
properly,
local interactions are irreversible,
and can be placed in a scheme of
entropy/negentropy,
such that the statistical mechanics approach
allows for a tensegrity that constructs the
properties of invariance,
and the contingency of living interfaces can be
then given category theoretical frame.

gnOme is a secret press specializing in the publication of anonymous, pseudepigraphical, and apocryphal works from the past, present, and future.

"They also remain elsewhere" (Luce Irigaray).

gnOme is acephalic. Book sales support the authors.

GNOMEBOOKS.WORDPRESS.COM

Other titles from gnOme

Annabella of Ely • *Poems: I-LXXVII*

A & N • *Autophagiography*

Brian O'Blivion • *Blackest Ever Hole*

Cergat • *Earthmare: The Lost Book of Wars*

Eva Clanculator • *Atheologica Germanica*

Ars Cogitanda • *footnote to silence*

M • *Un-Sight/ Un-Sound (delirium X.)*

M.O.N. • *ObliviOnanisM*

Pseudo-Leopardi • *Cantos for the Crestfallen*

I. P. Snooks *Be Still, My Throbbing Tattoo*

Rasu-Yong Tugen, Baroness De Tristeombre • *Songs from the Black Moon*

Subject A • *Verses from the Underlands*

Y.O.U. • *How to Stay in Hell*

HWORDE

Nab Saheb and Denys X. Arbaris • *Bergmetal: Oro-Emblems of the Musical Beyond*

N • *Hemisphere Eleven*

Yuu Seki • *Serial Kitsch*

Made in the USA
Las Vegas, NV
28 December 2021